Clean Eating

The No Calorie Counting Guide

Matthew Ward

© **Copyright 2016 by Matthew Ward. All rights reserved.**

This document is geared towards providing exact and reliable information in regards to the topic and issue covered. The publication is sold with the idea that the publisher is not required to render accounting, officially permitted, or otherwise, qualified services. If advice is necessary, legal or professional, a practiced individual in the profession should be ordered.

- From a Declaration of Principles which was accepted and approved equally by a Committee of the American Bar Association and a Committee of Publishers and Associations.

In no way is it legal to reproduce, duplicate, or transmit any part of this document in either electronic means or in printed format. Recording of this publication is strictly prohibited and any storage of this document is not allowed unless with written permission from the publisher. All rights reserved.

The information provided herein is stated to be truthful and consistent, in that any liability, in terms of inattention or otherwise, by any usage or abuse of any policies, processes, or directions contained within is the solitary and utter responsibility of the recipient reader. Under no circumstances will any legal responsibility or blame be held against the publisher for any reparation, damages, or monetary loss due to the information herein, either directly or indirectly.

Respective authors own all copyrights not held by the publisher.

The information herein is offered for informational purposes solely, and is universal as so. The presentation of the information is without contract or any type of guarantee assurance.

The trademarks that are used are without any consent, and the publication of the trademark is without permission or backing by the trademark owner. All trademarks and brands within this book are for clarifying purposes only and are the owned by the owners themselves, not affiliated with this document.

Disclaimer: This book is for informational purposes only. Use of the guidelines in this book is a choice of the reader. This book is not intended for the treatment or prevention of disease. This book is also, not a substitute for medical treatment or an alternative to medical advice.

Table of Contents

Introduction v
The Calorie Counting Concept 1
Clean Eating: The Core Principles 5
How to Start Clean Eating In 7 Easy Steps 7
The Essential Clean Eating Nutrients 10
The Unsung Clean Eating Nutrients 19
How to Stop Counting Calories: The Strategy 27
Easy No-Hassle Foods 30
Putting Your Meal PLAN Together 44
Bonus Section 46
Conclusion 50

Introduction

This book has comprehensive information on how to lose weight and improve your health without counting calories while on the clean eating diet plan.

You may be wondering, "What in God's name is clean eating, and does it imply your current diet is 'dirty'?"

Well, to begin with, we eat too much junk and processed food, and ingest too many chemicals. This is not clean eating. Have you ever thought of how many disorders, well, those you are aware of, that directly connect to an unhealthy diet? What comes to mind? Obesity, diabetes, hormonal imbalances, and different types of cancer, are just some of the diet-related ailments that spring to mind when we talk about 'dirty' unhealthy diets.

Clean eating is not about a healthy diet per se; it is more of choosing a healthy lifestyle that fosters optimum health. Clean eating is the simple practice of avoiding refined and processed foods and basing your diet on nutritious whole foods while engaging in any activity that fosters proper health.

Clean eating is more than choosing the right foods; it is about creating a proper nutrition structure in a bid to manage disease, avoid the development of diseases, remove toxins from the body, and lose excess weight (if there is any).

Clean eating as a very simple concept; it considers your food's path from its place of origin before landing on your dinner table; clean eating, and in extension, losing weight is not about becoming a calorie-counting junkie; it is more about looking at the nutritional value provided by the specific foods in your daily diet. While on a clean eating diet plan, your #1 priority is focusing on nutrient dense foods. Of course, this doesn't in any way mean that you eat foods that taste bad; a clean diet features healthy foods that are satiating. Think about it; while on a clean diet, you will be eating such foods like plant-based proteins like beans or animal-based proteins such as dairy, eggs, and meat, carbohydrates like bananas, polenta, rye bread, peas, brown rice, barley, whole-wheat pasta, beans and lentils, baked potatoes, and oats etc.

And the good news is that you really don't have to count calories while on the diet even when you want to lose weight. Counting calories does not guarantee weight loss. In fact, counting calories without properly planning your food intake or knowing why you are doing the math in the first place, will never lead to weight loss. So how does clean eating lead to weight loss anyway? Well, this book will show you how clean eating can make you lose weight and attain good health. It will give you a realistic, easy-to-follow plan that you can follow for the rest of your life. Unlike other diet plans that require you to be on the diet for a very short time (say 2 weeks to a few months), clean eating is more of a lifestyle diet in that after you start being on this diet, you don't stop- you live on the diet for the rest of your life. You stay on this diet plan even if you've attained your weight loss goals! Of course, given that you have the rest of your life to be on the diet, you cannot really be counting calories every single day; you have a life anyway! With the demands of this life, carrying around a digital scale everywhere you go is definitely not going to be practical; you can't be carrying a digital scale even when going on board meetings, going on a vacation and when going on surprise dates with your loved ones! But even with that, this doesn't mean that you cannot eat clean! This book will show you just how to adopt a clean eating diet plan.

Clean Eating

Before we get to discuss the specifics of the clean eating diet plan, let's start by understanding the concept of counting calories.

The Calorie Counting Concept

Losing weight comes down to knowing the amount of calories you consume in a day. Depending on your lifestyle, to lose weight, you have to eat lesser than the optimum calories per day depending on your daily calorie requirements. For instance, if you are a man, supposed to eat 2,500, to lose weight, you have to eat about 500 lesser calories per day to lose 1 pounds per week; keep in mind that this is entirely dependent on your lifestyle.

All foods, irrespective of their nature, whether processed or unprocessed, provide your body with calories: your body runs on calories. However, not all calories are equal. For instance, compare calories present in French Fries (these are what we call empty calories and are present in most processed foods) and compare them to calories in a healthy food such as Spinach; the differences are vast.

When you eat empty calories (these are calories present in all carbohydrates and unhealthy fats), it spikes your blood sugar levels. Your body will then use what it needs in that immediate moment. While these foods often have no other nutritional value, the body metabolizes the calories it does not immediately need into fat and stores them for future use.

Fat storage in the body is not a bad thing (stored fats can keep you warm and provide your body with energy when it is running low). However, excessively eating foods rich in empty carbs, as is the case with eating 98% of all processed foods, causes a wide range of ailments. For instance, the constant spikes in blood sugar cause an unhealthy digestive metabolism (type II diabetes is a good example of an ineffective metabolism), while the incessant fat storage leads to rapid weight gain and the development of ailments such as obesity and other lifestyle diseases.

This is where clean eating comes in. As we indicated, clean eating is about making healthy lifestyles choices inclusive of those related to your diet and lifestyle. To live a healthy life in every sense of the word, substitute foods rich in empty carbs. We are talking about foods like white bread, fries, and other 'white' foods such as white rice, pasta, and white flour-based foods with a healthier alternative such as legumes, brown rice, wheat pasta, veggies, and other healthy foods.

While you have to be mindful of how much, and which types of foods you eat, healthy, clean eating is not about counting calories. You may be wondering, "But you said losing weight boils down to reducing calories? Does it then not hold that to eat lesser calories, you have to count them?"

Yes, and no; 'yes' in that, losing weight boils down to either eating lesser calories or ensuring your daily activities cause a deficit in your body's calorific needs. For instance, if you are a man living a sedentary lifestyle, to lose about a pound per week, you need to eliminate about 500 calories per day (eat 2,000 calories). On the other hand, if you eat the same amount of calories, but exercise by going for a 4-5 mile run per day (running a mile burns about 124 calories), you will still achieve the calorie deficit (124 X 5=620, or 124 X 4= 496).

The 'no' comes in here in that to lose weight; you do not necessarily have to count calories; you merely have to be mindful of the foods you consume and make healthier lifestyle choices. That may sound contradictory; therefore, let us outline reasons why compared to healthy eating and adopting a healthier lifestyle, counting calories is an ineffective way to lose weight or ensure a healthy lifestyle.

Calorie Counting: The Ugly Truth

The reasons below, and many others, outline, why calorie counting is not as effective as the many blogs advocating for calorie counting, may have led you to believe:

Labels Can, And Often Lie: labeling laws legally allow a 20% margin of error on the nutritional facts panel. This means that the calories label on your snack pack could read 100 calories while the said snack has 119 calories.

Nutrients Vary by Season Ripeness and Variety: Food companies are in no position to analyze the nutrients value of foods including the calories present in every variety of food from every growing region with different growing conditions and all other variables. They probably have standards they will always refer to, despite the changes in the products nutritional value. You as a consumer will not be able to tell the difference.

Restricts Consumption of Healthy Foods: Focusing on calorie counting confines your food choices. For instance, high-fat foods have more good than just having a higher number of calories. High-fat foods have benefits such as absorbing antioxidants from vegetables, helping you stay fuller for longer, and getting necessary nutrients such as fat-soluble vitamins. When you count calories, i.e. avoiding foods you deem containing 'higher calorific value', you will overlook these benefits.

Counting Calories Is Too Much Work: Honestly, most of us will find it hard to find the energy and time to calculate all that we put into our mouths. You will probably need to have a digital scale; a scale you cannot take everywhere. Moreover, logging your food calories into your smartphone app becomes a waste of time.

Calorie monitoring increases your psychological stress; chronic stress deranges everything from your skin to your gut flora, to your immune system. If your diet leaves you stressed, it undoes the health benefits of the diet itself.

From the above, counting calories is clearly fruitless. Calorie counting can take off pounds in the short term but in the long term, those pounds will come right back. Instead of counting calories, create a more realistic diet plan consisting of foods that taste great and are more satiating; this approach is not only effective at weight loss, it is also great for your health. At this point, what you need to sustainability lose weight loss is a diet that:

- Addresses your hormonal and metabolic problems, thus making sure the food you consume goes into immediate use as energy instead of being stored as fats.
- Encourages a healthy way of eating instead of just thinking low in calories.
- You can see yourself following for the rest of your life.
- A diet that does not make you hungry, stressed, or miserable

Clean eating fits the above description, thereby qualifying it as the lifestyle to live. Clean eating has some core principles you should follow:

Clean Eating: The Core Principles

Clean eating is all about making healthy food choices and not counting calories. To this end, to get started on your clean eating journey, you have to follow the key principles as outlined below:

Cook Your Meals: Instead of buying processed meals that are likely preserved using chemicals, opt to cook your meals. Even if you feel it might take more time, personally preparing your meals is safer than eating processed meals and allowing them to siphon your health.

Eat Whole Foods: Basically, whole foods are foods that have not undergone the processing process in a manufacturing plant or lab. They are foods that you get straight from the farm; they include whole vegetables, fruits, free-range meat and grass-fed, whole grains, unsalted nuts, low-fat dairy products, and seeds.

Avoid Processed Foods: Processed foods are labeled foods; Foods made from more than one ingredient, with some ingredients you cannot pronounce. Do yourself a favor and kindly stay away from processed foods.

Eat Five To Six Meals A Day: Eating small meals regularly throughout the day will rev up your metabolism. When you eat six meals a day, you will never get hungry and will never feel deprived or feel the need to 'cheat' by binge eating a sweet dessert. Eating six meals a day keeps you from skipping meals or overeating, besides keeping your blood sugar and energy levels steady.

Combine Proteins With Carbs: When you eat a meal or snack, make sure the meal is balanced. For optimum satisfaction, and to ensure you are less tempted to eat junk food, combine carbs with protein and fat. This simple act will fuel your body and squash hunger pangs.

Watch out for Salt, Fat, and Sugar: Watching your salt, sugar, and fat intake should not be a problem once you cut out the processed foods responsible for excess calories and high level of sugar, fat, and salt. The clean foods you chose should be naturally low in all these ingredients.

How to Start Clean Eating In 7 Easy Steps

As we indicated earlier, adopting a clean diet does not have to be a stressing ordeal; in fact, as you shall shortly see, to adopt clean eating, all you need are the 7 steps outlined below:

Step 1: Establish Your 'Why'

Clean eating, just like any other habit, requires some effort. It is, therefore, important to establish what is inspiring your change. The motivation to inspire change should come from within and be rooted in positive thinking.

If you are cleaning up your diet because someone has told you to, or because of the guilt your current eating habit bring, know that this not a powerful enough motivator because they can always be influenced by someone or extenuating circumstances.

Step 2: Determine Your Commitment Level

Research shows you can develop new habits in just 21 days. In reality, when you really want to make meaningful real life changes, it may take months or even more. After thinking about your 'why'; then think about your level of commitment and devotion; here, think about how much commitment you have to plan your meals, and grocery shopping, to personally preparing and cooking your food. Doing these things could mean missing your favorite TV program to prepare healthy lunches or ditching your favorite fast food restaurant for whole foods. How much are you willing to give up?

Step 3: Do a Thorough Current Diet Audit

You could be thinking you are currently on a healthy diet. However, how healthy is it? Get a food journal. More often than not, we will think our diets are perfect until we see what we are consuming. Use your new food journal to keep track of what you have been eating in the past three days. Then make two simple lists:

- ✓ Foods that are nutritious and are not in your current diet
- ✓ Foods that are not healthy and that you want to eliminate from your diet; these could include sugary snacks, fast food, soda, etc..

Doing this will help you gauge your starting point and identify any emerging eating patterns.

Step 4: Choose Your Targets Wisely

The Pareto Principle applies in many areas of our lives including when you change your unhealthy lifestyle to a clean one. The Pareto Principle states that 20% of your efforts will lead to 80% of your results. Set small fewer goals you can consistently work on instead of trying to do everything at once. This is a more effective approach because small wins emanating from small goals can add up fast. Choose one habit per month and simply add on from there.

Step 5: Make Your Goals Specific and Measurable

If you bluntly say you are going to reduce the amount of cookies you eat, then yes, you will have your goal but it will not be specific. Make your goal specific by, for instance, saying your goal is to tackle your evening cookie obsession. To be more specific and make your intentions measurable, tell yourself you will keep all your cookies in the freezer and only take out one per day.

Step 6: Shop with a Purpose

Create a grocery list and stick to it. Clean eating is likely to put a dent in your wallet but that does not have to be the case. Looking for in-season produce and buying in bulk are two simple tricks you can use to manage your food budget.

Step 7: Meal Preparation

Start by searching for recipes that are simple and that you can quickly prepare. You can find lots of inspirations on healthy foods blogs or install an app on your smartphone to do the recipe for you. For plenty of leftovers, prepare your healthy food in extra-large batches so you can store or freeze for future use.

When adopting clean eating, you are likely to want more when you experience success. Set evaluation time and check your progress every single week. Did you somehow lose focus along the way, or are you still chasing your goal? Keep working on it until it becomes manageable and effortless. When the effort is gone, it means you are ready to take up the next challenge, a step that will move you closer to a clean eating diet.

The Essential Clean Eating Nutrients

The idea of consuming a healthy diet is one that each one of us learns from a very young age. When you adopt a clean diet, make sure you get sufficient amount of the following nutrients:

Proteins

Proteins are the most important nutrients for weight loss and a better-looking lean body. Proteins come from two different sources: they could be plant based such as beans or animal based such as dairy, eggs, and meat.

It is important to pay attention to what specific protein rich food brings on to the table when choosing protein sources. For instance, vegetable sources of protein will come along with healthy fiber, vitamins, and minerals.

How Much Protein Do You Need?

In excessive amounts, proteins can still lead to weight gain much like eating excess fats or carbs. The amount of protein you need will differ depending on your age, gender, and your current state of health. It is best to spread your protein intake throughout your day by eating it with every meal. As an adult, you need up to 3-protein servings per day. This is an equivalent of ½ cup of nuts or seeds, 1 cup of milk, 2 eggs, or 65grams of cooked lean meat.

5 Reasons Why Proteins Are Good For Weight Loss & Health

It is undoubtedly clear that proteins are a super food; other than providing your body with the nutrition it needs, below are more reasons why you may want to consider infusing more proteins into your diet.

Proteins Are Satisfying and Reduce Your Food Intake: At the beginning of your weight loss journey, proteins are important because they help you stay fuller for longer. Proteins are highly satiating because they slow down digestion thereby leading to reduced hunger and appetite, thus preventing the temptation to go back for second servings. This makes it much easier to control your food intake. If this happens more often, you are bound to lose weight.

Digesting and Metabolizing Proteins Burns Calories: Proteins have a higher thermic effect of food (TEF) when you compare them to carbs and fats. The TEF is the energy we use to digest food into small absorbent components. When you eat proteins, your body burns more calories during the 'metabolization' process.

Proteins>Carb Highs and Lows: Pairing protein with foods rich in carbohydrates slows down sugar absorption in your bloodstream. This prevents the levels of your blood sugar from hitting the roof and prevents incessant future cravings.

Proteins Promote Muscle Repair and Growth: You need to increase your protein intake especially after bouts of intense exercise. Right after your strength training session, consider having a protein snack because right after exercising, your muscles are sensitive to nutrients they can use to repair and grow.

Proteins Fuel Fat Burning: The truth is, your body does not have the ability to burn fats effectively for energy if it does not have help from proteins or carbohydrates. As you lose weight, your body loses both fat and muscle. It is important to add more protein to your diet during this process. Enough proteins coming from your food will fuel the burning of fats, and at the same time, preserve your calorie burning muscle.

Today, clean protein is hard to get. Finding clean proteins becomes almost impossible when you account for all the pesticides, antibiotics, and heavy metals present in all factories that produce non-organic meat, fish, dairy, and eggs.

To avoid the negative effects that come with the preservatives added to increase the shelf life, befriend farmers at your closest farmers market. At restaurants, ask questions to know where your food is coming from and go for the following foods whenever possible.

Ideal Sources of Proteins

Cage Free Eggs: Are rich in riboflavin, many important vitamins, and phosphorus. Eggs can be easy-to-digest foods if the chicken they came from had a healthy diet and were free-range. Whole eggs are nutritious because egg yolks contain most of the omega 3 fatty acids, antioxidants, minerals, and vitamins. Do not buy mechanically separated egg whites because they undergo chemical alterations. Instead, buy whole eggs.

Wild Fish: Not all fish are equal. When counting nutritional value, the origin of a fish matters a lot. Farmed fish are the same as caged chicken: both do not feed on natural food, are often sick, and probably full of antibiotics and dioxins. If you consume fish on a regular basis, go wild. Wild fish will contain many desirable omega-3 fatty acids

Quinoa: Quinoa is a complete protein pseudo-grain that is easy to cook. You can substitute buckwheat with this grain.

Organic Chicken: Chicken contains all the essential amino acids your body needs to remain healthy. The chicken in this subject matter is free-range chicken reared outdoor and raised in humane conditions and fed on a variable diet.

Grass-fed Beef: Grass-fed meat is rich in zinc, iron, and all the amino acids. It is cleaner, more flavorful, safer, and loaded with more nutrients if you compare it to grain fed meat.

Chia seeds: These seeds are a good source of calcium and phosphorous, and a very good source of dietary fiber and manganese. Chia seeds offer a complete protein that is mildly anti-inflammatory, and easy to cook and digest.

Hemp seeds: HEMP contains about 30% protein. 65% of the total protein content of hemp seed comes from globular protein Edestin, which our body easily digests and absorbs.

Lentils: Lentils are not a complete protein, but they are a great source of filling fiber, healthy carbs, and amino acids.

Cottage Cheese and Greek Yogurt: Plain cottage cheese and Greek yogurt can be a good addition to your balanced diet if you are not sensitive to dairy products. Cottage cheese and Greek yogurt are both low in sugar content and have a good amount of protein and healthy fats. Go for organic cottage cheese and Greek yogurt to avoid hidden fats chemicals and other artificial hormones.

Whey Powder: You will mostly find this protein in meal replacement powders, protein powder, and ready-to-consume milk drinks. Whey powder contains all the essential amino acids and glutamine. Ensure your preferred choice of whey is grass-fed, organic, and hormone free.

Pea and Rice Protein Powder: This powder is among the best combination of proteins available. The product is 80-90% pure and an easily digestible protein.

Spirulina: This super food is approximately 65-71% complete protein in its natural state. The protein in Spirulina is unique in its special way. It is up to 95% digestible. While it is great, make sure your chosen product comes from a clean water body.

Carbohydrates

Carbohydrates are our main source of energy for essential bodily functions like breathing and the beating of our hearts. An ample supply of carbohydrates is, also, necessary in the sustenance of our health. Hence, consuming sufficient amounts of carbohydrates is non-negotiable if our goal is to lose weight. One important thing to realize is that we cannot healthily shed weight by eating proteins alone. It is important to combine sensible portions of good quality, lean protein with clean good quality carbs in every meal to help you achieve and maintain a healthy weight. Eating a diet packed with the right kind of carbs is the secret to weight loss.

Misconceptions about Carbs

The misunderstanding about carbs often relates to its effect on our blood sugar levels. Understanding this is what will help you know its effects on weight loss. To begin with, there are two types of carbohydrates: Complex and simple carbohydrates. When you digest both, the body metabolizes them into blood sugar and releases them into the bloodstream, which we then use as fuel for normal daily activities and essential body functions.

Simple carbohydrates are easily digestible and cause a rapid surge in blood sugar levels. Your body's response to simple carbs is releasing insulin in large amounts to restore blood glucose levels by driving glucose into most cells. The body will then use the glucose driven into the cells for energy, stored as glycogen, or converted and stored as fats.

However, our bodies have a tendency to overreact and produce large amounts of insulin for large surges of glucose produced. Eating many simple carbs results in the release of insulin with 'highs and lows'. The lows are associated with dizziness, fatigue, weakness and hunger pangs, and cravings.

Excess insulin, also, inhibits fat loss by activating lipoprotein lipase, a fat storage enzyme that acts as a roadblock for the removal of fats out of the fat cells. Above all this, insulin inhibits hormone sensitive lipase, an enzyme responsible for breaking down stored fats.

For efficient weight loss, you might want to keep your insulin levels as even as possible. You can achieve this by limiting your simple carbohydrates intake as much as possible. For this case, simple carbohydrates will be in the **'dirty carbs'** category. Bad carbs sources include white bread, cakes, crackers, muffins, lollies, sugar, sweetened soft drinks, white rice, and biscuits.

On the other hand, complex carbohydrates will be the **clean carbs**. They take long to digest and are therefore able to provide you with a more controlled release of blood sugar. You, therefore, end up experiencing sustained levels of energy without moments of highs and lows.

Complex Carbs: Why You Must Include Them in Your Diet

Here are detailed reasons why you need to include clean (complex) carbohydrates in your diet for weight loss.

Carbs Fill You Up: Most food full of complex carbs will act as appetite suppressants. Complex carbs are more filling than proteins and fats. The body digests these special carbs at a slower rate than any other types of food, making both your brain and your belly feel full typically for up to 3 hours.

Carbs Will Control Your Blood Sugar and Diabetes: You can eat all the complex carbs you want, but you need to combine them well so you do not cause sugar spikes in your bloodstream.

Mixing the right carbs is the best way to control your blood sugar and prevent diabetes. Eat brown rice instead of white rice and combine it with corn, beans, and other foods high in resistant starch that will keep your blood sugar levels balanced -that is the beauty low carb diets.

Carbs Will Speed up Your Metabolism: Like proteins, resistant starches contain high amounts of carbs that speed up your body's natural fat burners including your metabolism. As complex carbs move through your digestive tract, resistant starch releases fatty acids that encourage burning fats while preserving your muscle mass at the same time.

Clean carbs include bananas, polenta, rye bread, peas, brown rice, barley, whole-wheat pasta, beans and lentils, baked potatoes, and oats.

Fats

You do not have to eliminate all forms of fats your diet to lose weight. Good fats do not make us fat; they maintain our body weight and promote good health. Fat is also a major source of energy and helps our bodies absorb vitamins.

Fats have a good amount of calories; therefore, controlling their intake is one of the most important steps in losing or maintaining weight and preventing type II diabetes. Our bodies only need a certain amount of fats per day. If you consume more than needed, the extra ends up being stored in the fat tissues resulting in weight gain.

Fats fall into two categories: healthy fats and unhealthy fats. Healthy fats include mono-saturated fats, poly-saturated fats, and omega-3 fatty acids. Omega-3 fatty acids are 'heart friendly'. They have the ability to lower high triglyceride levels in your blood. Omegas 3s are present in canola oil, flaxseed and flaxseed oil, walnuts, tofu, and organic fish. Mono-saturated and poly-saturated fats are also 'heart friendly' fats and can improve the level of cholesterol in the blood and promote weight loss. You can get these fats from avocados, nuts and seeds, olive oil and olives, peanut butter, and vegetable oils.

Saturated and Trans fats are the unhealthy category of fats. Saturated fats mainly come from foods that come from animals such as meat and dairy. They are present in some fried foods and some packed foods. Saturated fats increase 'bad' cholesterol level in our bodies, which in turn increases the risk of heart disease. Basically, many of the saturated fats are usually solid in nature. Some of the common sources include; butter, whole-fat milk, and cream, high-fat cuts of meat, high-fat cheeses, ice cream and ice cream products, palm and coconut oils.

Trans fat is liquid oil turned into solid fats during food processing by hydrogenation. Some Tran's fats naturally occur in some dairy products and meat. Tran's fats elevate your cholesterol levels by increasing 'bad' cholesterol and decreasing the 'healthy' cholesterol. To avoid Tran's fats, look on nutrition labels for such ingredients as "partially hydrogenated" or shortening.

Mono-saturated fats, poly-saturated fats, and omega-3 fatty acids, therefore, stand out as the clean fat safe for weight loss.

The Unsung Clean Eating Nutrients

Other than the essential nutrients discussed in the previous section, below are unsung, but highly beneficial nutrients you must include in your clean eating diet.

Water

Water is an essential part of our lives because it is responsible for proper blood circulation. Levels of oxygen in the bloodstream are greater when your body is well hydrated.

The body will burn more fats for energy when it has more oxygen readily available. Your body cannot make good or efficient use of fats it has stored for energy without the presence of oxygen. When it is well hydrated, your body will burn more fats because of the increased oxygen level caused by proper circulation of blood:

The Importance of Water in Your Diet

Just to mention a few, here are some of the reasons why you need to include water in your diet.

Water Is Life: We can only go for a maximum of 3 days without water. Water is a miracle cure for many of our common ailments such as fatigue, headaches, and joint pain, among many others. A mere drop by 2 percent in your body water can result to you having fuzzy short-term memory. We must constantly add water to our bodies to keep it properly hydrated.

Water Source: There is no other source of water in our body other than the water itself. Alcohol and soft drinks are among the 'bad' foods that steal a tremendous amount of water from our body. Other beverages such as tea and coffee are diuretic and all they do is get the water they got in out.

The Body Is 80% Water: Water makes up 80% of our blood, 85% of our brain, and about 75% of our lean muscle; we need a lot of it in our diet.

Water Transports and Metabolizes Nutrients: Water is essential for digestion, nutrient absorption, and chemical reactions in our bodies. Water metabolizes and transports the proteins and carbs our body uses as fuel.

Water Aids In The Toxin Removal Process: Water aids in the process of removing toxins from our body especially from the digestive tract. Water also suppresses our appetite and helps the body metabolize stored fat: two important reasons why water is important for weight loss.

Water Prevents Chronic Cellular Dehydration (CCD): Failure to drink water regularly can result to what's referred to as chronic cellular dehydration. This refers to a condition where your body cells do not get enough water making them vulnerable to attack from diseases because of their weakened state. CCD weakens your body's overall immune system and leads to chemical, nutrition and PH imbalances that can host diseases.

Finally, water regulates your body's cooling system especially during prolonged and vigorous exercises.

A general recommendation is to drink eight 8-oz. cups of water per day, making a total of 64 ounces, which is equivalent to about 2 liters or half a gallon of water. This is a generalization since our actual water needs depend on our diet, physical activities, and the climate. We need to provide our body with its minimum water replacement requirements by drinking the amount of water half our current body weight in ounces. For optimal weight loss, aim at drinking a gallon of water every day. This is equivalent to 128 ounces or sixteen 8.0z cups well spread throughout the day; drink this even when you are not thirsty.

Drinking water all day long can give you a sensation of fullness without consuming beverages high in calories like juice, milk, or tea with milk. Drinking a glass of water before meals will also cause you to eat less because it gives you the sensation of being full. As a result, consuming less food every day can help speed up weight loss.

Replacing artificially sweetened drinks with water further aids weight loss; this involves switching from 'dirty' drinks high in calorie content to a zero-calorie beverage.

Vitamins and Minerals

With all we have said, a balanced diet rich in carbs, proteins, and fats, is not complete without vitamins and minerals. Eating the right combinations of these foods will help shift your body into fat melting mode from fat-storage mode. Specific vitamins and nutrients can help flip an internal switch signals cells throughout your body to burn more fats and waste more of them as heat.

One way to lose the extra weight for good is by making good use of these critical fat-melting vitamins minerals. A myriad of vitamins perform many different functions in the body. Finding the right mix of minerals and vitamins to help with weight loss can be confusing.

Most of the time, an imbalance of important nutrients in the body is the reason you might have problems shedding the extra weight. Discovering your mineral deficit and replacing them with the necessary nutrients can kick start your body into losing weight.

Types of Vitamins to Help You Lose Weight

While you should aim to get a sufficient amount of all critical vitamins and minerals, while adopting a clean eating diet for weight loss purposes, below are the vitamins you should include in your diet:

Vitamin D: Vitamin D is the most notable weight loss vitamin. We have the ability to process vitamin D when we expose our skin to sunlight. This vitamin is also present in dairy foods, fatty fish, and in supplement form.

GLA-GLA works by increasing metabolism and reducing stress. You can find this vitamin in plant-based oils; in large amounts, you can find it in hemp oil, primrose, and evening hemp oil. The daily limit for adult GLA intake is 3000mg per day.

B-Complex: B-complex vitamins are groups of vitamin that help your body metabolize fat. They work in your body as enzymes that burn and mobilize the stored energy in foods. They also assist indigestion, which helps your body rid itself of nutrients it does not need. These vitamins appear to be the best for weight loss because they also produce a feeling of fullness that curbs your appetite thus reducing your food consumption rate.

Thiamine: This vitamin helps break down carbohydrates; you can find it in wheat germ, bran, rice, and beans.

Riboflavin: You will find this vitamin in organ meats, yeast, eggs, rice, brewer's yeast, milk, mushrooms, spinach, broccoli, and whole grains.

Choline: By using cholesterol to prevent weight gain and reduce weight gain, choline works as a fat emulsifier. It is plenty in seafood, eggs, chicken, collard greens, and turkey.

Chromium: Chromium works in the body by breaking down carbohydrates and fats that increase energy, which aids in burning fat. Chromium plays a significant role in the utilization of insulin and regulation of insulin and blood sugar. You will find it in most cereals and grains.

Replacing a poor diet with clean foods and supplements packed with nutrients is the first step to halting the overeating cycle. Some vitamins help burn fat by increasing the metabolism. Certain nutrients found in foods and supplements reduce stress. When you feel stressed, the brain then sends a signal to rest of the body to start storing fats especially as your anxiety levels rise. Lowering your stress levels usually inhibits the body's mechanism for storing fats as well as enables your body to burn a lot more fats.

Vitamins pills and supplements are often the only reasonable way to add the necessary missing nutrients into our diets; however, the best way to consume these vital nutrients is by eating them in their natural state. This is best for weight loss because most of the foods packed with vitamins will keep you full throughout the day. A good example of such a food is broccoli.

Note: If you are looking forward to using supplements to lose weight, be very careful and avoid overconsumption of supplements. Pills and capsules with high amounts of nutrients can be deadly if you take them at a toxic level.

Fiber

Fiber, also known as bulk or roughage, is a carbohydrate you will find in fruits, vegetables, whole grains, and legumes. Our bodies do not easily digest this special kind of carb. It passes quickly through your system, relatively intact, without causing a rise in your blood sugar and reducing the risk of type II diabetes.

Fiber is classifiable as either soluble or insoluble. Soluble fiber dissolves in water forming a gel-like material. You can find it in oats, barley, psyllium, carrots, citrus fruits, apples, beans, and peas. It has the ability to lower blood cholesterol and glucose levels.

Insoluble fiber does not dissolve in water. This type of fiber promotes movement of material through our digestive systems and improves stool bulk. Wheat, bran, bean, nuts, whole-wheat flour, and vegetables such as green beans, cauliflower, and potatoes are a good source of insoluble fiber.

Fiber: Its Core Benefits to the Body

A high-fiber diet will benefit you in the following ways:

It Will Normalize Your Bowel Movement: Dietary fiber will increase the size and weight of your stool and soften it. A bulky stool will decrease chances of constipation because it is easier to pass. Fiber helps loose watery stool solidify by absorbing the water and increasing its bulk.

It Will Lower Cholesterol Levels: Soluble fiber you get from beans, flaxseed, oats, and bran may help lower the levels of the 'bad' cholesterol thus lower total blood cholesterol.

It Will Help Maintain Bowel Health: A diet high in fiber will lower your risk of developing small pouches in your intestines and hemorrhoids.

It Will Help Control Your Blood Sugar Levels: If you suffer from diabetes, doubling your fiber intake can slow down sugar absorption and improve your blood sugar levels.

All fruits and vegetables contain fiber with most of it concentrated on the skin, seeds, and membranes. To lose extra pounds and stay healthy, women under the age of 50 years should aim to get 25 g of fiber a day, while men should aim for 38 gram a day.

When it comes to losing weight, fiber simply helps you feel full without the need to add extra calories to your diet. When you eat a baked potato inclusive of the skin, you are less likely to feel hungry an hour later; compare this to when you eat a bag of potato chips.

How to Stop Counting Calories: The Strategy

As we have consistently seen, to shed off those pesky pounds, you do not necessarily need to count calories, you merely have to make healthier diet and lifestyle choices. In this section, we shall outline how to stop counting calories, while making weight loss work.

The Portion Size Method

We need to have an idea of how much we eat per day so that we can adjust our needs and weight loss goals accordingly. However, calorie counting is not the best approach to use.

The portion size method will save you the trouble of carrying around measuring cups and weighing scale, and the need for smartphone apps. Your hand is a portable and personalized tool you can use to measure your food intake. All you need are your hands; regardless of the size, and an ability to count and you are good to go. Here is how it works:

- ✓ Your thumb will determine your fat portion
- ✓ Your cupped hand will determine your carb portion
- ✓ Your fist will determine your veggie portion, and
- ✓ Your palm will determine your protein portion

    (Every portion will be the same thickness and diameter with the part you are using to measure.)

To determine your proteins intake for protein-dense foods like beans, dairy, eggs, fish and meat, two palm-sized portions is the recommended portion with each meal for men. For women, one palm-sized portion is usually enough.

To determine your carbs intake for carb-dense foods like starches, grains, and fruits, women will use 1 portion of cupped-hand sized with most of their meals. 2 cupped-hand sized portions of carbohydrate is the standard portion size for men.

To determine your vegetables intake for veggies like carrots, salad, spinach, or broccoli, use the two fist-sized method for portions of vegetables is the recommended portion for men. On the other hand, women will only need 1 fist-sized vegetable portion with every meal.

To determine your fats intake for fat dense foods like nut butters, seeds/nuts, butters, or oils, 1 thumb-sized portion of fats is the recommended portion for women in most of their meals. Portions for men will be 2 thumb-sized fat portions with most meals.

Clean eating requires you eat 5-6 meals in a day. This usually boils down to 3 main meals and 2 or 3 hefty snacks. This should prevent you from skipping meals or overeating. It also keeps your blood sugar levels steady. You now have a simple and flexible guide to planning your 3 main meals based on the meal-sized portion.

For women, use the following portions for your meals:

- ✓ 1 entire thumb of foods dense in fats
- ✓ 1 cupped hand of foods dense in carbs
- ✓ 1 fist vegetables

Clean Eating
- ✓ 1 palm of protein dense foods

For men, use the following portions for your meals:

- ✓ 2 entire thumbs of fat dense foods
- ✓ 2 cupped hands of foods dense in carbs
- ✓ 2 fists vegetables
- ✓ 2 palms of foods dense in protein

As you can see, this method is nearly as accurate as counting calories, and it is much easier too.

Easy No-Hassle Foods

In this chapter, you are going to learn where you can get quick clean foods without the hassle of having to cook.

Protein

When a person feels satisfied from their personalized eating plan, they're far more likely to stick to it. However, it is not like you are able to break out a grill in the car to cook you up a healthy protein filled meal or snack. Here is a list of protein-rich snacks that involve no cooking whatsoever.

Cottage Cheese: This offers 20 grams of protein for every five ounces. If you think that Greek yogurt is the best for protein, then you should think again. One serving of non-fat cottage cheese has three more grams of protein in it that a serving of Greek Yogurt. Bonus, it will give you 125 milligrams of calcium.

Hard Boiled Egg: Eggs used to be considered to be bad for you; however, nutritionists express that eggs are extremely good for you. But only if you eat them in moderation. Nutritionists say that an egg for breakfast is considered to be the powerhouse of breakfasts. Along with protein, eggs offer you a great dose of vitamin D, as well as vitamin B-12 per egg. The greatest part is that they are extremely easy to take with you anywhere. All you have to do is peel them before you eat them. Some stores even sell already boiled eggs if you do not feel like going through the cooking process.

String Cheese or Mini Cheeses: These offer you 6 – 8 grams of protein for each serving. There are personal packages of different cheeses like Sargento sticks or Mini

Babybel. These are amazing if you want to take them with you. You can even choose part-skim.

Edamame: These offer you ~ 8 grams of protein in just one-half cup. In addition to the filling protein, they also offer three grams of fiber. Eating them roasted is also a great option.

Roasted Chickpeas: This tasty snack offers you seven grams for just a quarter of a cup. It can also lower the LDL cholesterol levels. You can make your own just by rinsing the chickpeas in a bowl with some olive oil. Use your choice of spices like cumin, chili powder, salt, and pepper. Bake them in your oven at 425 degrees Fahrenheit for 45 minutes.

Greek Yogurt: This type of yogurt has 12 – 20 grams of protein in each container. If you are aiming to get more protein, then this is a great option. Greek yogurt is strained; therefore, it has a thick consistency. It also has more protein at half of the sugar than a traditional yogurt. Depending on the type of brand you purchase, you will get about 12 to 20 grams, as well as calcium and probiotics.

Whole Grain Protein Bars: These will give you about 10 to 15 grams of protein. The nutrition bars are a great idea. They are very filling and very easy to take with you. However, before you consume these, read the labels very carefully. Some of them are packed with fat and sugar. You will need to aim for one that has 10 to 15 grams of the protein with about 5 grams fiber, and 15 grams or lower of sugar. One good one is Luna Bars.

Turkey Roll-Ups: Turkey roll ups give you about 18 grams of protein. A great snack that you can prepare and put in a baggy is a slice of turkey that has a strip of mustard, slice of tomato, and a leaf of lettuce. Inside. You can even pump this up by adding a few baby carrots or even a thin slice of red pepper. This combo offers you ~ 18 grams of protein.

Low Fat Chocolate Milk Box: These offer you 9 grams of protein. Chocolate milk is a great post-workout snack. It gives you 9 grams protein and will help you repair muscle and improve the recovery time. You can purchase single serving boxes of the low-fat milk from different companies like Organic Valley. They do not need to be refrigerated. You can put one in your purse or gym bag.

Hummus Cups: Hummus is made from chickpeas, olive oil, and tahini that have been pureed. The hummus is a great and healthy snack that offers fiber as well. You can even make your own and add in carrots, grape tomatoes, red bell peppers, or even cucumber.

Tuna Pouches: Each pouch of tuna will offer you 16 grams of protein. It is a pouch, so all you have to do is tear it open. There is no draining necessary. All you need is a fork. Each of the packets has 16 grams protein and offers 100 percent of your daily need of antioxidants. If you do not love the taste of tuna, then you are able to purchase marinated flavors like lemon pepper.

Kefir: This is a drinkable type of yogurt that offers 11 grams of protein for every one cup. It is very creamy, and it has three times the amount of probiotics in comparison to typical yogurt. It also offers vitamin D. It does not contain lactose.

Peanut Butter Pack: These offer 8 grams of protein for every 1.15 ounces. You would not want to put a jar of your favorite peanut butter inside your purse, but you can use the packs for convenience, as well as a great source of protein. You are able to purchase individual packs of nut butters. They keep anywhere like purses, bags, backpacks, and more. There are some that have no sugars added as well! You can even eat it on a banana. The banana will give you antioxidants, as well as fiber.

Almonds: You can eat 14 almonds for four grams of protein. You can purchase a bag and separate them, or just carry the bag with you wherever you go. You can even purchase the 100 calories almond bags to take with you. To add to your snack, you are able to add in dried fruits like pineapple or apricots. This will give you more fiber as well.

Carbohydrates

Fruits: Fruits are great because most, naturally, are the right size when using the portion size method strategy of eating. You can take these as snacks anywhere hassle-free. When it comes to the smaller fruits such as strawberries and blueberries measuring them with the strategy is very quick.

Dry Oatmeal: Oatmeal is great to mix in with cottage cheese, yogurt, or even protein shakes! You can also take the traditional route, portion out your serving size, and add water or milk.

Sweet Potatoes: This's a delicious option that also works extremely well with the portion method. All you have to do to make these a hassle free food is to poke holes, with a knife or fork, in the potato, wrap it in a paper towel and put it in the microwave for a short amount of time.

Canned Beans: If you don't have time to cook beans the traditional way then that's not a problem! Canned beans are another great option for your carb sources. Just heat them up for a short amount of time and you're ready to eat in minutes.

Veggies

The great thing about veggies is that you can eat most of them raw and make great snacks. You can bag them up and take them with you. If you go the frozen veggie route, then it just a matter of sticking them in the microwave for a short time and you're ready to go!

Spinach

Broccoli

Clean Eating

Green Peppers

Cucumbers

Tomatoes

Red Bell Peppers

Carrots

Garlic

Onion

Fats

Most of the foods that contain healthy fats were covered in protein; however, to make it simpler here is a list of the foods that will give you the healthy fats that your body needs.

Avocados

Cheese

Dark Chocolate

Whole Eggs

Salmon

Mackerel

Trout

Sardines

Herring

Walnuts

Almonds

Macadamia Nuts

Chia Seeds

Extra Virgin Olive Oil

Coconut

Coconut Oil

Clean Eating

Meal–Prep Your Food

In this chapter, you are going to find out why buying in bulk and cooking your foods in advance is a time, money, and health saver.

Those who have felt the vice grips on their bank accounts have turned to bulk buying. Costco saw a seventeen percent increase in sales within just one year. The pros of buying in bulk offer savings since it is less money per unit. If you purchase a large enough size, then you can freeze or store the rest for later use without having to purchase more. You will also have to visit the store less. You save time and gas.

Tips for Buying Bulk

You may want to organize the pantry and freezer before you go grocery shopping for your bulk products. Consider purchasing containers or baggies for organizing as well.

Think about what you go through fast when it comes to groceries and make a list. This list will help keep you on task when you go to purchase the money saving items.

You will be freezing a lot of your bulk foods to ensure that they remain in good condition by the time you unfreeze them for the preparation of meals.

Here is a list of great items that you should stock up on:

Teas

Coffee

Sweeteners

Oil

Clean Eating

Rice

Almonds

Seeds

Poultry

Beef

Carrots

Celery

Avocados

Bell Peppers

Cereals

Yogurt

Chickpeas

Oranges

Grains

Beans

Lettuce

Spinach

Eggs

Hummus

Cheeses

Cottage Cheese

Milk

Potatoes

Prep Your Foods to Keep Eating Healthy

The most common excuse is, "I do not have time,". Well in this section you are going to learn to make time.

As much as everyone knows how important it is that you stay limit their trips through the drive-through, fast food window, people still rush to be in line for that grease dripped burger. When you have had a long day or you're on the go, then you're more inclined to get foods that are less healthy than you should be eating.

Eating clean can be a bit of a challenge at times, especially once you are away from your kitchen. Research suggests that if you plan ahead, you will be more successful when wanting to follow a specific diet. Here is a look at many different ways that you can make meal preparation work for you and your new way of clean eating.

Pick one day a week when you are able to grocery shop for the week. Also, set a couple of hours aside in order to cook the foods that you purchase for the week.

Turkey or Chicken Breasts

The good old chicken breast sits in the center of most diets. These are able to be purchased in a bulk bag. Depending on the rest of your meal, these are able to be eaten hot or even cold.

Clean Eating

- Cook the turkey or the chicken right after you buy it. Even if you are not going to eat it in the next 2 to 3 days.
- You will need to marinade it if you want to do it this way. After you have cooked it, you can keep it in the fridge for 3 to 4 days in the refrigerator. You can also freeze it individually in baggies or one big bag.
- For a meal, you can add your choice of carbs and fats.

Rice

Cooked rice will last ~ 2 days in the refrigerator, or you can freeze baggies of it and heat it up when it is time for you to eat it. You can add it to your chicken or your turkey.

Eggs

Eggs are a great snack and breakfast. You can boil the eggs and keep them in the refrigerator for two to three days. Make sure that you are boiling them within a couple of days of purchasing them. You can add them to stir-fries, eat them as a snack, or add them to spinach salads.

Chopped Vegetables

Vegetables are extremely versatile. In addition to them being used for soups, salads, and stocks, they are amazing for snacks and meals. They are inexpensive and a great way to offer great nutrients for your body. You can purchase them in bulk. Chop them or slice them. Put them into baggies; dividing them up into meals. Put them in your freezer and defrost them using the microwave. You can cut the vegetables into bite-sized pieces and put them in baggies. They will keep for a week. Most frozen veggies come bagged, cleaned and cut already!

Soup

Soup is a great candidate for the freezer. Make a big pot of your most favorite healthy soup that is not creamy. Allow it to cool and then pour it into bags or microwave safe containers. You can use the microwave to heat it up. You can even heat it back up on the stove if you want to.

Ground Turkey

Ground meats can be prepared far in advance to save time and eat clean. You should brown the turkey and drain it. You can cook enough of this for the week. Allow it to cool off some and then put it in meal sized baggies or a container. Put them in your freezer. It will last a long time. You can defrost it in your microwave and use it for many meals like stir-fry, tacos, chili, or other dishes that you love.

Summary of Bulk Cooking

Once a week you will need to purchase your vegetables and your meat in bulk. Brown your ground turkey, chop up your vegetables, and then put all of it into small baggies or containers. Put these prepped foods in your freezer. Put your chicken into a marinade if you want and pop it in your refrigerator.

Keep a couple of hours aside one day every week. During that time, grill (grilling is a great option for cooking bulk) your chicken for a few days, make a very large batch of your favorite soup and freeze it. Before you go to work every 2 – 3 days, boil six eggs and you can use them for snacks or to add to meals.

Food Safety Tips

Do not re-use your chicken marinade. If you do not use all of it, you need to get rid of it. You will cross contaminate, and the chicken juices will spoil very fast.

Clean Eating

Make sure that you always wash your hands after you have handled raw meat. Make sure you do not use the same surface to cut chicken and vegetables. Wash the surface with soap when switching foods or use a new surface. The same goes for knives and other utensils.

Make sure that you put your leftovers away right after you are through with them. Keep them completely covered. You will allow them to dry out or allow them to grow bacteria if you don't.

Putting Your Meal PLAN Together

Example of a day's meal plan using the portion size method would look something like this:

Meal 1: Rye bread+ Soy milk+ purple cabbage + roasted peanuts

Meal 2: Corn +Mexican salad + Beans +Avocado

Meal 3: Diced potatoes + chicken + olive oil + broccoli

Meal 4: Banana+ hemp+ asparagus + Sushi slice

Meal 5: Salty lime roasted nuts + chocolate chips + blueberries + baked potato

Meal 6: Baked oatmeal + granola + apple slice + olive oil

You can start here; however, if you feel you need less food because you:

1. Are trying to lose weight
2. Are not very active
3. Are not getting weight loss results
4. Eat more frequently all day
5. Are feeling too full at meals
6. Are smaller in stature,

Start by removing ½ thumb of fat and or a ½-cupped handful of carbohydrates from a few of your meals every single day if you are a woman. For men, remove 1 thumb of

Clean Eating

fat and or 1 cupped handful of carbohydrates from a few meals every single day.

If you feel the need for more food because you:

    1. Are trying to gain muscle and are not getting enough muscle result

    2. Are very active

    3. Eat less frequently all day

    4. Feeling satisfied at meals

    5. Larger in stature

Start by adding ½-thumb fat and or a ½-cupped handful of carbohydrates to a few meals every single day if you are a woman. For men, add 1 thumb of fat and or a 1-cupped handful of carbohydrates from a few meals every single day. This is a starting point. Be free to make any adjustments basing on how it works out for you.

Bonus Section

Cheat Days

A cheat day is a day of the week you eat 'bad' without having to worry about the nutrition content of what you are eating. Cheat meals should not spell doom to your clean eating lifestyle. In fact, if you structure them well, they can help you lose weight. It is totally okay to cheat, on condition that you do not overdo it.

Why You Need to 'Cheat'

First, you occasionally need to feed your soul. No foods can substitute, at least from an emotional standpoint, the crispy French fries, the cold refreshing cold bottle of coke, or the cold beer bottle you love dearly. These foods bring you memories and when you cut them all out, cravings can drive you nuts. Occasionally feeding your soul by taming your cravings will keep your mind and body at ease.

Second, cheat foods are good for your metabolism. They keep your body guessing about what to expect next. When this happens, your body does not get comfortable with how it burns its chemicals and continuously works hard to figure out new ways to function so you do not store fats.

Finally, having cheat meals will help you have a more positive relationship with food. The foods you label 'bad' are often the ones you crave. By having cheat days, you teach yourself how to handle being around tempting foods. Cheating also protects you from developing disorders like binge eating. In fact, cheating is a more realistic approach instead of eliminating these foods in your life forever.

When to Cheat

Clean Eating

Choose one day of the week as your reward day; go for Fridays, Saturdays, or Sundays because they are easily interchangeable. When your cheat day beckons, be careful not to ignite your old bad eating behaviors.

Cheating Tips

- ✓ Only have a cheat day if you have been honest with your meal plan the whole week.
- ✓ Do not make too much of your cheat meal that you feel tempted to store some for the next day. Have enough for that day so you do not have to test your mental strength.
- ✓ Make smarter cheat meal choices. Do not get crazy and get into food comas. Have limits; for instance, if it's drinking beer, do not exceed 3 if you are female or 5 if you are male; anything more than that and you will be stalling your weight loss.

Matthew Ward
Non-Meat Protein Options

Meat is what normally comes to mind when one thinks of protein, as all meats offer protein. However, if you want to eat meat-free or if you want to become a vegetarian, then you need to be armed with the right information.

Meat that is not prepared will cause food-borne illnesses like salmonella so you need to consider other types of food sources or even supplements in order to get the protein that you need. The Centers for Disease Control and Prevention expresses that you should eat 10 to 35 percent of the daily calorie intake. You are able to get adequate quantities of protein without having to fry up a steak or other protein source. Here are some steps that you can do to add some protein into your diet.

- ✓ Consume some dairy products that are high in protein. Drink 1 cup of milk. It has eight grams of protein. Purchase some low-fat yogurt that has fruit, as an eight-ounce serving. It has 11 grams. Eat some cottage cheese, Parmesan, cheddar, or mozzarella.
- ✓ Add in nuts and some seeds to your meals. Medline Plus expresses that sunflower seeds, almonds, hazelnuts, peanut butter, and walnuts are great for protein. You can eat some nuts for a protein packed snack. They even have healthy fats. You can purchase granola bars that have dried fruit or some mixed nuts.
- ✓ Bean sprouts or grains are great to eat. Rinse the seeds or the grains thoroughly, and then just soak them in some water as the instructions state. Drain them or dry them to eat. Consider quinoas, they are a seed that is similar to rice. It doesn't require you to cook at all.

Clean Eating

- ✓ Avocados, as well as coconuts, have great protein content. You can eat them raw or even as a part of a meal that is raw.
- ✓ Eat salads that are high in protein. Put in some seeds, nuts, dairy, and beans. It will offer you a tremendous amount of protein and other important vitamins.
- ✓ Drink smoothies and shakes that offer high protein. You can use soy or whey powder to mix into drinks. Mix it in milk or whole grain cereals like oats. Make sure to read the instructions.

Things you will need:

- ✓ Milk
- ✓ Protein Powder
- ✓ Seeds
- ✓ Yogurt
- ✓ Fruit
- ✓ Vegetables

Conclusion

When it comes to dieting, the best plans are not complex; they are simple. Clean eating and the portion size method is applicable to anyone who is ready to change his or her lifestyle and physique. The benefits of adopting a clean diet are many; besides being an easy lifestyle to lead, it will help you shed those extra pounds without necessarily worrying about calorie counting. Well, truly, anyone can measure how many carbs, proteins, and fats to take by using their hands- it is just easy to follow irrespective of where you are. The diet plan is just too simple for you to fail while at it especially given that you are not aiming for perfection as well as the fact that you can customize the diet plan for your unique needs i.e. there is no standard eat-this-don't-eat-that except for the guidelines we've discussed!

The truth is; you don't need to aim for perfection whether you are starting out or have been on the diet plan for years because when you obsess about perfection, you will lose out on the simplicity that comes with eating something just because that's how you've chosen to live.

I hope this book was able to help you to understand how to go on a clean eating diet plan.

The next step is to just start! There is never a perfect time to start and you really don't need to be perfect at it. All you have to do is to be consistent with whatever it is you've committed to do and then watch how stress-free your weight loss journey becomes.

Thank you and good luck!

Made in the USA
Middletown, DE
02 December 2016